Proceed With Awesome

A Poetic Voyage

by

Following Whispers

Chapter and Verse Publishing

Copyright © 2018 Clinton Burns

First published in 2018 by
Chapter and Verse Publishing

All Rights Reserved. No part of this book may be reproduced in any format, print or electronic, without explicit permission in writing from the copyright owner.

ISBN 978-1-9164627-0-0

To find out more about the author, this publication or their other work, go to
followingwhispers.com

Dedication

This book of poetry is dedicated to my Moma, who showed me that love is real, helped me understand that it can come from the smallest seed in the harshest conditions, and that it will only grow if you continue to nurture it, in the hope of a better tomorrow.

Contents

Introduction: Clearly Awesome	1
Birth	6
The Truth Is Out There	7
The Wonderful Ride	8
Good, Bad and Normal	9
I Really Don't Know	10
The Mighty Lightning	11
Together Again	13
Secrets of The Crescent Moon	14
Rain Drops	16
Bad Experiences of Obsession	17
True Love	19
Infinity	21
True Love (Pt. 2)	23
Pressure	25
True Love (Pt. 3)	27

The Search For True Love	29
Change	31
Moma	34
Malice	36
Beginning's End	39
Truthful, Hurtful, Vicious Circle	41
Goodbye Already	44
Lost In Translation	48
Natural Intoxication	59
...But It's Christmas	62
Concrete Parasite or Paradise	67
The World Is So Cold...	70
Grateful	72
Not Really Worth My Time!	77
Sometimes But a Shadow	80
About The Author	83

Clearly Awesome

Hello, and welcome to my think space. The following collection is the first chunk of a linear time-line of poetry that I wrote, with the sole purpose of putting my experiences and emotions into context, whilst recording the most pivotal milestones and life-affirming moments of my existence.

I have always been a very introspective and sensually attuned character, my head is and has always been swimming with ideas, thoughts, observations, feelings, doubts, love and much more besides, but before I began writing, they had no real expressive outlet, I simply bottled them up and battled with the pressure that they exerted on me.

The thing that eventually ignited my desire to become a poet, was an emotional struggle that knocked me for six. In my very early teens, I lost my Uncle on Boxing Day, aged 32. Around three months later, my Biological Father died, a man I grew up without any knowledge of, only meeting him in a Father-Son context a mere 5 weeks before he was no more. I also found out during being told who he was, that there was very good reason for him not being part of my life.

These and other difficult situations, were left to fester for a couple of years inside my noggin, before I finally began to confront them, whetting my scholarly whistle in my first poem, 'Birth', which is featured in this very text. Do not be fooled by its simplicity, having fully embraced my 'Geekdom' just prior to this moment in my life, I ensured that there was a lot of substance hidden between the lines, as is the case with most of the poems featured in this book, and those I have yet to publish.

Ultimately, 'Birth' opened my eyes to the fact that there was a tool I could use to clear my head, and comment on my own pain, other varied emotions, communicate my perspective and also be explicitly decisive on how I wanted to proceed, all transcribed with as much transparency or guise as I decided to employ.

At this point in my life, I was on my way to achieving the realisation that beauty could be born out of not only love, but also pain and other motivations. The more I used this therapeutic implement, the more I realised that it helped me to find a silver lining in even the darkest emotions, experiences, observations and topics; find positivity even in the face of extreme negativity; find strength when I was being forced to feel weak; and find hope that my tomorrows would be brighter. The other, albeit unplanned benefit from penning these personal narratives, is that the poems have helped others to achieve the same things, just by reading them and applying them to their own lives and experiences. Safe to say, I was hooked.

I have never attempted to force a poem, only ever putting pen to paper when I feel literally electrified with inspiration. The select handfuls of people I shared them with prior to presenting them in book-form have enjoyed them immensely, and their excitement in my musings helped fuel my ambition to eventually begin publishing them, so that I can show people that are feeling isolated that they're not alone; to inspire them to turn things around for themselves; to feed and nourish their hopes for the future; and to encourage them to fill their lives with people, experiences and things deserving of the title AWESOME!

The late, great author and poet Maya Angelou, said it best when she declared, *"my mission in life is not merely to survive, but to thrive; and to do so with some passion, some compassion, some humour, and some style."*

The poems featured in this published work span a decade of my life, and I would like to invite you to join me on this first segment of my journey of discovery, as I began making sense of life, death, love and everything in-between.

Another inspirational figure of mine, the dearly departed superhero Nelson Mandela, gave some insight into what drove and motivated him when he said, *"courage is not the absence of fear, it's inspiring others to move beyond it."* With that being said, an all too familiar phrase echoes this sentiment, when it states that, *"fortune favours the brave"*, so I highly recommend that you too... **Proceed With Awesome!**

Birth

The Mother's womb is the place of all birth,
Before you contradict me, please think first,
The Universe is the womb of all planets,
Except the making of planets is completely man-less.

Some planets are made, but never born,
The first signs of life break the uterus wall,
After that, the planet does fall,
And supports itself, to be adored by all.

As the planet does grow old,
The same old story is to be told,
As one planet enters the tomb,
Another is forming in the womb.

The Truth Is Out There

As we look up into space,
We know we're not the only race,
We watch life cycles take their place,
The wondrous truth we can't embrace.

We all were once made from the dust,
Chafered from the Earth's thick crust,
With aliens we make a fuss,
Did we find them, or did they find us?

Scientists cheer, but they haven't a clue,
They look for beings like me and you,
I warn them all, watch what you do,
We don't know who is after who!

The Wonderful Ride

Girl, you are so understanding,
Though sexually you're so demanding,
You're in my room, you hit the deck,
You're sexy, I say what the heck.

You stick out your tongue, I take the hint,
I've got the gas, you've got the flint,
Together we make an eternal flame,
This is no longer a simple game.

My hands start to wander, I play with your breasts,
On a deeper level, we're put to the test,
We're both in the mood and we're feeling alright,
Now we can have pleasure for the rest of the night.

We both get prepared, the protection's applied,
We both want it, so I slip inside,
We're both on cloud nine, we just want to glide,
Afterwards you whisper, *"what a wonderful ride"*.

Good, Bad And Normal

I want to make this poem formal,
And express the meanings of good, bad and normal,
Of things good and bad, the World is full,
If there's no bad, then good is normal.

After good, then comes bad,
After bad, people are glad,
Without bad, things could never improve,
After you've had bad, you've nothing to lose.

We must have a mixture of bad and good,
For without one of them, our lives are a dud,
People who have lives so enchanted,
Take the good things all for granted.

They don't see, with all their greed,
A mixture's what they really need,
Mixtures are needed, just look at our blood,
It's normal for a bit of both bad and good.

I Really Don't Know

Whatever I do, I'm always wrong,
My surroundings show that I don't belong,
No matter what happens, I can't do the right thing,
I never know what my next action will bring.

I feel so bad inside, though I just want to sing,
With my emotions I'm inside a wrestling ring,
The directions I take, whatever move I make,
I feel like I've finished my happiness cake.

There's nothing left, not even a crumb,
I've started to think that my heart has gone numb.
I don't know to who, or where to turn,
And whenever I breathe my stomach does churn.

I've turned to the left, I've turned to the right,
I've even stayed up in sorrow all night.
Where to now? Where can I go?
What can I do? ...I really don't know.

The Mighty Lightning

Bright and sharp,
Its strength is so great,
In its charged hands,
It has everyone's fate.

Even royalty bow,
To its fearsome might,
In awesome anger,
It strikes in the night.

Lightning will shatter,
Whatever is under,
But isn't as ferocious,
Without its friend thunder.

Together they creep,
From place to place,
They have the power,
To destroy a whole race.

When up against it,
Don't put up a fight,
If you want to be vaporised,
Go fly a kite.

If you really know,
What's good for you,
You'll deeply respect,
The lightning too.

Together Again

When I see you, I just want to say,
When can you come to my bedroom and play,
I picture your legs, your sexy physique,
Your wonderful breasts, and your firm, fit ass cheeks.

I see your cute face, your smooth silky lips,
You've a perfect body, and I love every bit,
We had so much fun, those times were pure bliss,
You've got a great voice and a breath-taking kiss.

I wish we could once more be together,
And when we kissed, we'd brighten the weather,
Together we'd make an explosive bond,
Your juices would flow at a wave of my wand.

We'd have such strong feelings, we just wouldn't care,
We'd have so much pleasure, we'd both get grey hair,
Throughout our lives, these memories will last,
So let's get together and make some more fast!

Secrets Of The Crescent Moon

The moon has many faces,
Each one is like someone,
Things we see, and things we don't,
Of those times now long gone.

Some people keep lots locked away,
Some people will share most,
But no matter how open they might be,
There's one door that stays closed.

Everyone has a dark side,
Even if not shown,
And if they do share most times,
It's when trust has grown.

Inside myself, I hide things too,
Of times I wish I could forget,
Things I couldn't tell a soul,
Though one day this I may regret.

As I went to bed last night,
Upon my pillow was moonlight,
The light, distinctive and so bright,
I looked and saw a truthful sight.

The moon it smiled and called my name,
I saw myself, and it was right,
I guess there's only me to blame,
That half was black, and half was white.

Rain Drops

See them start falling down from the sky,
They come and engulf all that is dry,
If you've no protection, when rain clouds are full,
They'll jump off the edge and land on your skull.

Your clothes can't stop them from hitting your skin,
Unless you've a coat, they'll always get in,
If you're caught off guard, this you could regret,
As you may get a cold from getting all wet.

Some people admire them, some people do not,
I love their cool touch, though some prefer hot,
If I need a lift, they will always help,
As I love the sensation of them on my scalp.

When I'm around them, my smile never ends,
That's why I call them my wet little friends,
It has to be said, they can be a pain,
But I generally love the drops we call rain.

Bad Experiences Of Obsession

Challenges, tests and assault courses,
Slicing through phases like butter and knife,
To desire, explore and then collate knowledge,
Are the segments of our occupation in life.

Stepping off treadmills, going through turnstiles,
Then coming to walls, barbed wire and fences,
Gripping, scrambling, trying to get over,
The things we call bad experiences.

Love is imitated by infatuation,
Lust exists, not a true loving bond,
As time passes, the falseness is obvious,
The victim can see that things are wrong.

You lose interest in their affections,
Like bad smells they still try to linger,
The end is proclaimed, but they're still attached,
Like super glue that's stuck to your finger.

Use warm water, have a good soak,
To make sure all traces of them are gone,
It's only when you're properly clean,
That you can be sure you're free to move on.

The last thing you need is someone obsessed,
Learn, then avoid it and let life unfold,
I've been there, done that, just washed the T-shirt,
You deserve the best, but you have to be bold.

If you're someone's partner and you're unhappy,
You need to break free, by picking the lock,
Then walk away without turning back,
And build your foundation as solid as rock.

You'll change as I have and inherit wisdom,
Through finally having learnt your lesson,
Build your relationships firstly on friendship,
Not mind games, violence, lust or obsession.

True Love

I want to tell you all about love,
And share its secrets and power with you,
The colour, the warmth and mostly the beauty,
Of a force that is strong when it's true.

I perceive it to be like a flower,
With pollen to share when it blossoms and blooms,
The pollen from one may inspire another,
Or sometimes it gets people high from its fumes.

Avoid fake flowers called infatuation,
These imitations should always be feared,
Although some people scarred from a past love,
Prefer things genetically engineered.

Me, I'm out there, after the real thing,
Planting seeds, only to see stunted growth,
My heart still awaits the growth of a flower,
As I promised it one, and I swore under oath.

There is a seed, and it has my name on,
Fairly nearby if I look hard enough,
That will grow into a large and prosperous flower,
If I plant it before life tries calling my bluff.

The seed bears a magnet, drawing me closer,
Whispering softly, though I don't know where from,
I just wish to find this pure divine power,
Before I blink and my time has all gone.

When this flower grows and matures,
My heart will be at peace for all time,
And the flower shall be wilted by nothing,
As I will have united with the power divine.

To every love searcher following whispers,
Don't wallow in pain, you must go beyond,
For if you stay focused and try to be patient,
I'm sure that you'll find your true loving bond.

Infinity

Travelling is something we all seem to do,
Either physically or exploring the depths of the mind,
Whether it's miles or thoughts that you cover,
You can't do it all in a single lifetime.

Just think how many square metres this World has,
Too many for any one mind to perceive,
It's impossible for someone to visit each metre,
And know that they've been everywhere when they leave.

All of the knowledge and information around us,
Could never be absorbed or viewed by one brain,
Those amazing facts of existence and culture,
For one person to know, would send them insane.

Complex data and ancient mysteries,
That place or fact the map or media missed,
Secrets, experiences and Government cover-ups,
Put together would form an infinite list.

There are people you shall never walk past,
There are things you shall never think of or see,
Things that don't interest you, so you miss out,
Wisdom you want that is never released.

This planet amazes me with what it contains,
I know I can never know its full contents,
Questions I have that shall never be answered,
Things that I've read, but don't get what they meant.

If you know everything then there are no surprises,
Being a know all, you'd have nothing to seek,
I'm glad that this is not at all possible,
As you'd be detained and labelled a freak.

We're a small, compact ball of information,
There is so much more away from our planet,
Stars, Galaxies and the unknown Universe,
We want this knowledge, but could we handle it?

True Love (Pt. 2 – A Losing Battle)

Love is all around me, its presence suffocates me,
I really think it hates me, instead of being elevating,
It's not uplifting like a friend, but occasionally pretends,
It waits until I'm off guard, then jabs my guts again.

I've done a lot of training and learnt how to box,
I'm stronger and faster, but still you penetrate my blocks,
You hit me in my head, my heart and my lungs,
Inflicting permanent damage, with no guilt for what you've done.

Your fuel is my desperation, to possess your benefits,
As long as I search for the myth, you will always exist,
You had me following whispers from the age of five or six,
It started off with a kiss, but now what I want is bliss.

If you were a human being I would never befriend you,
But when people offend you, all I do is defend you,
Protecting your name in vain, when you brought me such sorrow,
I guess its 'cause I think that you'll change your ways by tomorrow.

You never listen to me, instead you just abuse me,
Never stop, just pass through me, storming off in a rage of fury,
The only reason for this is because I'm not defeated,
Each time it hurts me more, but its just history repeated.

If I managed to recover then, I can still manage now,
I'm gonna continue to challenge you until to the day you stand down,
If you had a forehead you'd frown, 'cause my pain threshold's greater,
You can't win them all, you're gonna lose sooner or later.

So what is it to be, are you with me or against me?
Because if you're against me, I'll drain you 'til your empty,
I'll hammer the anger with honour, plus the mistrust and the lust,
Take away potentially painful stuff 'til all that's left is us.

My new role shall be the sculptor, I shall remould love,
And soon I shall have the power to do things unheard of,
You think you'll overcome me, well reality sucks,
You'll fulfil my expectations! You think not?!
Well GOOD LUCK!

Pressure

Do you know what your limit is?
How far would you go to get what you want?
If someone was pushing your head under water,
Would you wilfully drown, or show them they're wrong?

If they held the key to fulfilling your dreams,
But could also lock them away,
Would you struggle and squirm, or stand up, be firm,
And express what your heart wants to say?

You are the expert on your own performance,
Whether you can do better, or if you'll die trying,
If you've reached your peak and they still want improvements,
Be straight, say you can't, there's no use in you lying.

As long as you've gave it your best shot,
You've stayed true to yourself, there's no need to be down,
There's more than one ladder to get to the top,
Don't cling onto this one while they shove you down.

Take their fingers out of your ears,
So that you can hear and follow your heart,
It will show you how to get through this,
Or give you the options for a brand new start.

Don't be exploited, self-worth is your treasure,
Be honest and strong and your success will grow,
When the pressure's intense, I know my limit,
But my question for you is – do you really know?!

True Love (Pt. 3 - A Gardener's Dream)

A lovely lady with a beautiful smile,
Used to pass me by and say hello,
Her circumstances meant that I couldn't pursue her,
But we were unaware what the future would hold.

A special occasion with a friendly gathering,
Then off to a club for more fun and drinking,
I offered a dance to mark the occasion,
With no hidden agenda, just innocent thinking.

As we held each other, dancing away,
Intimate feelings seemed to be present,
I wanted this moment to last forever,
I looked in your eyes and I'm sure I saw heaven.

Could you be the seed with my name upon it?
The one that will grow, even in drought,
My heart believes that my oath has been honoured,
It's just what the whispers had told it about.

The seed has been planted, it's starting to stem,
A large and prosperous flower awaits,
Potential pain is defeated, I stand victorious,
As my heart has finally broken free from it's cage.

All I know is, my heart is yours,
Your heart is mine, we've earned each other,
From the deepest depths of my soul, I Love You,
I choose to be with you, I need no other.

The Search For True Love

Affairs of the heart are a complex subject,
I feel I'm an expert, but I don't know a lot,
Under favourable conditions it can be so right,
But my experiences are only of getting it wrong.

If it's not one thing, then it is another,
Some problems are foreseeable, others hidden well,
But whatever obstructions or dilemmas arise,
They secure your visit to the Heartbreak Hotel.

Hearts full of hurt, over-protected and insecure,
Navigate away from the path to love,
They want a smooth route that goes nowhere special,
Rather than one that does, with a journey that's rough.

The rest of us may become distracted,
Change directions or even get bumped off the road,
Most will break down simply because of…
Previous journeys, too much baggage, no way to unload.

Enough about journeys, lets list some problems...
Other men or women; lack of money or time;
Family pressures; children; jealousy; abuse;
Broken vows; lifestyles; lust; deceit; lies.

I've been the victim of most of these,
The baggage has been heavy and hard to carry,
But they will never crush my will to live and love,
I'll get my full flower and possibly marriage.

Until this time, I'll just keep on going,
Planting seeds, seeing stems and then decay,
As some seeds don't like the soil I reside in,
They need different conditions and just rot away.

I now need to concentrate on my survival,
My heart's cage has tamed me, I'm in danger when free,
Should I go back to the wild and search with caution,
Or still open the cage, but let them come to me?

Change

I have an extremely pressing matter,
Which seems to bewilder and interest me,
It's something peculiar that frequently happens,
And when it does many things rearrange,
It can be quite obvious and simple, but sometimes,
It lurks in the shadows and cannot be seen,
After much observation it's time to share,
My understanding of the essence of change.

What is change? What makes this occur?
These are both great questions with answers that vary,
The most common of these are a shift from the norm;
Progression; digression; something beautiful;
On one hand some people expect and except it,
While others fight against it or find it quite scary,
Whether it is natural, encouraged or forced,
In one form or another it's inevitable.

Another question that seems to arise is,
What is the outcome of such a transition?
The interpretation may differ mainly because,
The truth is in the eye of the beholder,

If it is valued and supported throughout,
It should reward you with an advantageous position,
Many positive things happen when looking forward,
But danger awaits those who look over their shoulder.

We need to use change to make thing improve,
By harnessing the positive realities possible,
With this strategy and constant encouragement present,
We can create personal and worldwide benefits,
Acknowledge that existence is far from rosy,
With invisible cages and so much that's horrible,
Lots needs to change for things to be fair and equal,
The light is here somewhere, will we ever see it?

If achievement is to be within our grasp,
We must have a proactive approach here first,
Drawing from the resources available to us,
Not wasting them as there are no second chances,
Our objective while on this continuous journey,
Is to change for the better and not for the worst,
Cherish the lessons of adverse outcomes,
They will guide future decisions to your advantage.

Change is like a molecular transformation,
Energy's expelled and can be lost or absorbed,
Positive emissions cause a chain reaction,
During which, a mass of goodness can come about,
With the right approach and mentality used,
It will shower you with numerous rewards,
Remember, if you want to make a real difference,
The best thing to do is to start with yourself.

Moma

What is this quiet and peculiar place?
Part of me knows, part of me does not,
Surrounded by darkness, but still I feel safe,
So comfortable, well fed and not cold or hot.

Where am I? ...well this is the start of my life,
Where I grow and develop, become big and strong,
I'm bored, but can't leave 'til the time is right,
Then out comes a gift weighing 10 lb, 1.

It's so bright out here that I can't see a thing,
I'm scared and alone and now my bum hurts,
I'm placed in your arms and you comfort me, smiling,
And I knew then that you were my whole Universe.

The truth back then, is still true today,
Such genuine feelings, no need to pretend,
Our bond is so strong, nothing gets in our way,
I could never love anyone more than my best friend.

You've made my World an enchanting place to live in,
Always there for me, to help break my fall,
When I think you can't love me more, you find a way of giving,
You're an excellent Parent, the greatest of all.

Having you in my life is a blessing,
I wish more people could know you the way that I do,
Instead they're content with not knowing, just guessing,
With fictitious assumptions, they haven't a clue.

You're a gem, a diamond in the rough, so precious,
But you let people exploit you, they don't know your worth,
Staying quiet, so as not to make any fuss,
Demand respect, don't be abused like the Earth.

No matter what happens, I will always be proud,
Whether you're 10 stone or 30, have brunette hair or grey,
You're a wonderful person who I can't be without,
My love for you grows each and every day.

Malice

I refuse to remain mute in this sensitive matter,
Your tongue used to lick, now it lets lies loose,
Once quick to please, suddenly it harms even faster,
With malicious accusations, distorting the 2Ruth.

I wish you wouldn't speak to or of me ever again,
Too much to ask as you shout and play the victim,
I can't believe you've got the nerve to see this as revenge,
When I only humiliated you for the things that YOU did!

All I did was love you, when you felt so alone,
Helped you through your problems, stopped you slitting your wrists,
Which I would never have done, if I had known,
My reward would be you acting like such a BITCH!

When your issues evaporated, you had to make new ones,
Why machinate to destroy your best hope for survival?
With intentions and words that are so Machiavellian,
Using smoke and mirrors, plus constant denial.

Never have I witnessed such a devious nature,
Misuse of position, or a soul so empty,
It can't be justified when you meet the Creator,
Why you caused devastation like W.M.D.

I have suffered my own internal 9-11,
It's not been one occasion, but several events,
Each with the impact of the war Armageddon,
Extremely one sided and severely intense.

I confided in you, of loved ones having suffered,
The true experience of what you now accuse me of doing,
Little did I know then, that my openness would,
Sow the seeds to later inspire the plot of my ruin.

The 2Ruth is I'm not ruined, just full of regret,
For letting you get close and showing compassion,
So you could bring me to tears with your lack of respect,
But Karma will make sure you pay for your actions.

You've murdered the B.F.G, not Fee-Figh-Foe-Fum,
I'm a tame and rare Tiger you've hunted and killed,
You've witnessed the damage, but still your tongue Burns,
Like the effect of sulphuric acid after it's spilled.

Despite this corrosion, you continue to pour,
A sick smile on your face, you clearly don't care,
A Mad Scientist without an ounce of remorse,
Bringing me and those near me, close to despair.

The Devil incarnate, and I put that lightly,
You LIVE but only by spelling it backwards,
You've a chemical imbalance, this is more than to spite me,
Making your lies stick by highlighting my Blackness.

Slanderous utterance by the tongue of a Serpent,
Yet after all this injustice, I still hold no grudge,
It won't be long now before I close your curtain,
Even if that means standing in front of a Judge.

Beginning's End

All that preceded led up to this moment,
The sponge had spent years constantly absorbing,
It did shed a few drops, but kept much of its content,
Knowing that this would eventually be very rewarding.

The time had come to show what it was made of,
Demonstrating its capacity, how much it can hold,
By wringing itself out, every last drop,
To resurface and then go back in like a mole.

See, the knowledge, the substance, maintains its value,
Not just as the final impression is made,
Followed by suspense as the contribution's reviewed,
Plus the hope that it's given a desirable grade…

1st Class, 2-1, I'd be happy with these,
Reimbursement for all of the effort and stress,
But I'm destined for greatness, regardless of their beliefs,
And have pride in the fact that I've given my best.

So what's left now, a life full of parties?
Heck No! Celebrations may last a few weeks,
Then it's time to set course, all-aboard me 'arties,
Navigation is simple... hear the wind as it speaks.

A predestined destination inscribed in the air,
Still most don't know where I'm heading, even some of my crew,
Many are short-sighted, unable to see what's out there,
But that's how they've chosen to construct their view.

By adjusting the scope, all ranges and opportunities are captured,
Blessed with this ability, I'm adept in many a task,
Advanced armoury and cannons ensure complete rapture,
I'm backed-up to the 9's and can reload real fast.

So don't bet against us, take heed to this warning,
Like cats we'll continually land on our feet,
Stronger, wiser, in-tune with our calling,
The odds and fake Gods are what we shall defeat.

Truthful, Hurtful, Vicious Circle

There she is, a pretty girl of 15,
Hooked on drink and drugs, living so obscene,
That's her life, she's never had any hopes and dreams,
And what worse, is she's already got a baby.

She's alone, there's nobody she can talk to,
Shown no love, instead her parents hug the corkscrew,
Down the pub, every minute they can afford to,
Looking back, her whole life has been so awful.

She got no support when she said that she was pregnant,
Instead, *"it's your fault, you should've used protection,*
You won't get any help from me, you must be jesting,
You were enough, this time I won't be stressing."

All this from the abuse of drugs and sex,
Not to mention her parents selfishness and neglect,
Such a heavy burden, she's constantly depressed,
A life with no joy, but overflowing with regrets.

Now we see, a young boy of 13,
From a broken home, single-parent family,
He gets away with more stuff than you could ever believe,
Hanging with a bad crowd, always up to mischief.

Family and friends have never told him this was bad,
No pocket money, so he chose to sell a 20-bag,
Thug father figures, due to the absence of his dad,
Made him cold-hearted, unable to feel sad.

His mother don't seem to care, plus she's only 28,
Never says *"be home by 8 and don't be late,"*
More like *"I'm off to the pub, your dinner's in the microwave,"*
So it's understandable that all he fears is the grave.

Lil' man, with the World upon his shoulders,
To feel safe, he bought himself a gun and holster,
With no supervision, flames started coming from the toaster,
Some sigh in relief at the death of another monster.

See what happens from a lack of love, care and awareness,
Who's to blame, him; his mother or grandparents;
Drug dealers; gun distributors or local thugs;
Biological father; community; police or government?

The fact is, they all played a part in this tragedy,
By being negligent and/or feeding the disease,
How do most of these people at night manage to sleep at ease,
When another teenager, by their hand is now deceased?

His mother and grandparents hug the corkscrew tighter now,
His so-called father doesn't know next week, his son enters the ground,
The dealers and thugs say, *"did ya see how shorty went out!?"*
The gun gets back to the distributor, who sells it to someone else.

The government and police turn a blind eye to it all,
"Gang-related, case closed, let's go patrol the football,"
Like lemmings to the slaughter, we're in for another fall,
Unless we admit we made the cycle and initiate its reversal.

Goodbye Already? Goodbye Already!

A: *Pssst! Whispers, are you there, can you hear me?*
Thought it was 'bout time I paid you another visit,
I know how happy you are whenever you're near me.
FW: I'm happy anyway, what do you want, what is it?

A: *Hey, don't be like that… it's your friend Alcohol!*
FW: I'm not sure if I would really choose to call you that.
A: *I've been the life of the party and down for the long haul.*
FW: Yeah, I remember when we met, man that was way back.

I was 5, experimenting with drinks at a party,
People thought I was drinking coke, I was… with Rum.
A: *Yeah, I always know exactly how to get the party started!*
FW: And ended, with a sore arse, when I was caught by my Mum.

How can you be proud of getting kids to drink?!
A: *I didn't force you, just satisfied your curiosity.*
FW: At that age everything's new, I think your morals stink!
A: *I don't like your tone, after all I've done for you, what a pity.*

FW: Well, I'm glad you brought that up… let's take a look shall we,
There are so many incidents I don't know where to begin!
A: *But you wouldn't have done half the things you've done without me.*
FW: I suppose you did help me to find the confidence within.

But you made me believe I could handle you, when sometimes I couldn't.
A: *That's your own fault for mixing me or going too fast,*
Just like the others, you got greedy, I'm fine in moderation,
But you still had fun, even if it didn't always last.

Because of me, look at the fine females you were able to screw!
FW: You sound like a Pimp man, plus I'm not your puppet!
A: *Well, I gave the really fit ones 'beer-goggles' when looking at you.*
FW: Thanks a lot! ...and what about when you embarrassed me in public?!

There were several times where I violently spewed my guts up,
In sinks and toilets, on people's shoes, even on my own clothes,
Not to mention all the damage you've done to my organs and stomach!
A: *Again, there's nothin' wrong with me, simply the method you chose!*

FW: Yes there is, you slowly attack people from the inside,
Some get addicted, some get violent, some become very ill,
A: *Well, if you abuse me, it's only fair you should die,*
FW: Tell that to the families of the millions you've killed!

And, don't think I've forgotten about my Uncle,
David, who you enticed and eventually stole from us,
May he rest in peace, because of you, he died so young.
A: *You all die at some point, I don't see what's all the fuss!*

FW: There we are, you're finally showing your true colours now,
People think you're harmless, so you get away with murder,
Government endorsed, socially acceptable, but in truth plain foul,
We've come a long way, but I don't want to know you any further.

It's time for me to go teetotal, I'm tired of your crap,
You were fun while I studied, but you're overdue erasure.
A: *I don't care what you say man, I know you'll be back!*
FW: I doubt it, but if it happens, I'll just remember this conversation.

Lost In Translation

These italic paragraphs serve as a preface,
To what could otherwise be a native speakers' nightmare,
As a precautionary measure, I included this in case,
It's hard to read, even for those who don't need eye care.

Originally assuming it was easy, my subconscious begged to differ,
Claiming the format was complex and would puzzle most readers,
At first, the thought of adding more to it made me bitter,
Until the poem became the baby, and I viewed this as the foetus.

The poem was written with a Polish lady in mind,
Who moved to Germany aged 7, from her native country,
Then to Birmingham at 19, not knowing what she'd find,
With one of her friends, but leaving behind Little Sis and Mummy.

She came here to improve her English and also find a career,
The first task was easy, but she had trouble with the latter,
An au-pair in the day, at night serving people beer,
But these were not the type of jobs to make her 'happy ever after'.

Frequently on the phone to her Mother, friends and family,
10 out of 10 for effort, but reality was lethal,
With no luck at the Job Centre, she switched to Plan B,
Then weeks later met a tall, dark man in a tuxedo.

It was me, it took a while to get her phone number,
We arranged to meet, and you'll find out what happened soon,
She had a glow about her like the crotch of Goldmember,
Yes, the baby won't be long now... its birth is almost due.

It will be bilingual, speaking (P:) Polish, (G:) German and (E:) English,
Detailing conversations, thoughts, actions and emotions,
With the resources at my disposal, I couldn't resist,
Having an echoing (T:) Translation throughout most of the poem.

I don't care if it's not perfect in its intended transition,
I spent 5 days researching and writing, just to say,
What I've decided and to justify my current position,
I can see the head, my message to her is only a push away...

(E:) This poem has been developed mainly because,
(G:) Ich kann nicht mehr leiden (E.T:) I can't stand it anymore,
(E:) I think this is not working! (it's become a dud),
(G.T:) Ich glaube dies ist nicht in ordnung!

(E:) I'm also pretty sure (G:) Es kann nicht repariert werden,
(E.T:) (I've given it some thought and think) It can't be repaired,
(E:) I could never have saw this coming, we're going backwards instead of further,
But have no specific regrets about the time that we've shared.

(G:) Ich weiss nicht genau (E.T:) I don't know exactly,
(E:) I simply feel like something is (G:) fehlen (E.T) missing,
(E:) It's apparent that something is (G:) manglehaft (E.T:) weak/lacking,
(G:) Ich sprechen mit gross aufrichtigkeit (E.T:) I speak with great sincerity.

(E:) I remember our first date, we covered many questions,
(G:) *Hast du geschwister?* Nein, ich bin einzelkind,
(E:) *Oh, you're an only child?!* Well, (G:) *ich habe eine schwester,*
(E.T:) *I have one sister* (E:) she seemed nice, when I met her on her visit.

(E:) After our first date I asked you (G:) konnen wir uns weidersehen?
(E.T:) Can I see you again? (G:) *Ja, was möchtest du machen?*
(E.T:) *Yes, what would you like to do?* (E:) It's up to you. Okay then.
I knew I'd enjoy spending time with you, regardless of what happened.

I was right, each time we met, more and more I thought (E:) I like her,
(G.T:) Ihr gefällt mir (E:) and you seemed focused on me like a lover,
We both went slow, but we could've been as swift as a deadly viper,
After a while though, I started to wonder (E:) could I have some sugar?

(G.T:) Darf ich etwas zucker haben? (E:) you gave me a little sachet,
But sometimes I couldn't tell if we were (G:) zusammen oder getrennt,
(E.T:) Together or separate (E:) when you're given consistant intimacy,
There's no need to question whether you're (G:) frei oder betsetzt.

(E.T:) Free or taken (E:) the mistake on my part was never asking you,
(G:) Wollen Sie mit mir ausgehen? (E.T:) will you go out with me?
(E:) Instead it was assumed, because I liked you, you liked me too,
We spent a lot of time together, chatting, laughing and kissing.

I made your (E:) 21st Birthday (G.T:) einundzwanzigsten geburtstag,
(E:) You didn't make my 23rd, which was a few days before,
I managed to enjoy myself and not take it too hard,
And had to say (E:) I'm sorry, unfortunately she can't come.

(G.T:) Es tut mir leid, leider kann Sie nicht kommen,
(E:) My friends and family would've liked to meet the lady in my life,
You said (E:) Thanks for the invite (G.T:) *vielen dank für die einladung,*
(E:) But you couldn't, as you were tired from working all night.

I let it slide, because it wasn't really your fault,
(G:) Sind sie frei am morgens? (E.T:) are you free tomorrow?
(G:) *Nein, aber haben Sie Mittwoch etwas vor? Wir können irgendwo etwas trinken.* (E.T:) (so you go)...

No, but are you doing anything Wednesday? We could, Have a drink somewhere! (E:) Sounds good, why not!
(G:) Könnten wir uns um Mittag bei die fünfzig bushaltestelle treffen?
(E.T:) Can you meet me at Midday by the 50 bus stop?

(P:) *Tak* (E.T:) *yes* (E:) we had fun, after, you said,
(G:) *Vielen dank für den angenehmen tag* (E.T:) *thank you for a pleasant day,*

(E:) We'd done most things except sharing a (P:) lóżko
(E.T:) bed,
(E:) But that was welcome at the time, just sort of the way...

I chose, I didn't want sex obstructing our foundation's harmony,
I didn't communicate this to you except in a poem of mine,
Didn't ask (E:) what would you like? (G.T:) was möchten sie?
(E:) Inside we both wondered (E:) will we have to wait a long time?

(G.T:) Müssen wir lange warten? (E:) after a while I thought,
(E:) Is there a short cut? (G.T:) gibt es einen kürzeren weg?
(E:) I asked if you'd stop at my (P:) dom (E.T:) house (of course),
(E:) Always (P:) *nie* (E.T:) *no* (E:) right there, I should've used my (P:) glowa (E.T:) head.

(E:) Instead I simply asked (G:) wann müssen Sie weider züruck sein?
(E.T:) What time do you have to be back? (E:) usual reply,
soon,

I couldn't begin to understand (G:) warum? (E.T:) why?
(E:) We'd start to get closer and then you'd seem to kill the mood.

The reason lay within an issue unforeseen by me, but simple,
Easy as counting from (P:) jeden (E.T:) one (E:) to (P:) dwa (E.T:) two,
(E:) Instead I quizzed myself (G:) was wünschen Sie? was muss ich tun?
(E.T:) (Insecurely) what do you want? what must I do?

(E:) My 'Mojo' is usually great, but started to seem ineffective,
Then I pondered (G:) habe ich genug? (E.T:) have I got enough?
(E:) At no point was there evidence that you were deceptive,
But was I just good entertainment or were you looking for love?

Like I said earlier for some time we've moved in reverse,
You'd applied for courses in Germany, and awaited replies,
Ready to leave so (E:) what are the odds! (G.T:) wie ist der wettkurs!

(E:) Of getting a possible reason to stay? Me walking into your life.

I wish I would've known sooner what you were dealing with,
Emotional tug-of-war for you, a similar effect for me,
Some confusion, causing distance, we pulled back a bit,
Don't you think? (G:) *ich bin einverstanden* (E.T:) *I agree.*

(E:) Recently, we've met less frequently and we're back to small-talk,
It seems most of the progress we made, simply went in a blink,
It's like I'm on a (E:) slippery surface (G.T:) strassenglätte (E:) and can't walk,
Similar to the time we ice-skated at Solihull Ice Rink.

I feel like water with all the qualities of freshness, but kept stagnant,
If I stay like this I'm not doing myself any favours,
I'll attract negativity, no (G:) glück (E.T:) happiness (E:) just badness,
I'm tired of thinking (E:) what can I do for you? (G.T:) was kann ich für Sie tun?

(E:) I've reached the ticket office, and pulled my wallet out,
Asked the assistant (G:) einmal nach Ledigdorf, einfach bitte,
(E.T:) One ticket to Singleville, one-way please (at least for now),
(E:) Payed the price for my request and now only await the ticket.

My temporary home will have a sign, (E:) trespassers will be prosecuted!
(G.T:) Unbefungten ist das betreten verboten! (E:) for a little while,
I'm still glad we met, the time we've spent, I've really enjoyed it,
But it's time to say (G:) aufwiedersehen (P.T:) do widzenia (E.T:) goodbye.

Natural > Intoxication

[Compose] ...*click* ...*opening,* ...*please wait,*
To: {Every contact in my address book},
Re: FW's Autumn Update,
Attachments: (1MB) [Enjoy the Rush].

Message: Hello World, I know it's been a long while,
Thanks for all the messages you've sent me,
I reckon you're overdue me dropping you all a line,
In my defence, I have been quite busy recently.

"Busy doing what?" I predict you'll wonder,
Busy being reborn (not the answer you expected),
Right now I seem peculiar, like the taste of cucumber,
But you're probably intrigued and find it quite perplexing.

Okay, enough of the stalling, now I'll clarify,
It's about me having given up drinking alcohol,
I remember when I did, everyone was asking *"why?!"*
Like I was defying a sacred protocol.

I gave most of my reasons for what I'd chosen,
Disowning Devil's Blood, with a poetical vow,
Most see it as unthinkable, like their brain's frozen,
It's really very simple, shall I show you all how?

I looked at what part it played in my life,
From the very first sip, to the last noxious guzzle,
It was by this process, that I was able to see the light,
Put together all of the pieces and solve the puzzle.

I realised I didn't need it, it did me no good,
A meaningless infatuation, with no solid rewards,
How can anyone let an alien reside in their blood,
Deform their whole existence and not eliminate the cause?!

So, in my case it finds itself estranged from its host,
No longer extracting my finances; intelligence or health;
I feel happier; smarter; stronger; I'm no longer broke;
And I was able to achieve all of this by myself.

All it took was a strong will; determination; discipline;
Some people seem to look at me like I'm Superman,
But these and other tools, we all possess within,
Don't doubt yourself, what I've done, anyone can.

A natural high is greater than alcohol intoxication,
Giving uplifting energy, a constant buzz, not peaks and troughs,
If you don't want to join me, it's your potential you're wasting,
But I won't pressure you, as you would me, it's your loss.

If you decide you too have had enough like I had,
Then take that first step and join the 'Natural Faction',
You can still go out, have a laugh, pull, have a good dance,
Basically, just follow the title of my email attachment.

Anyway, I've lots planned, so it's time for me to disperse,
I hope to hear from you soon, take care of yourself for me,
Loads of love and respect, Following Whispers,
[Send] ...*click* ...*message has been sent successfully.*

"...But It's Christmas!"

September, whoops, I mean December the twenty-fifth,
Holds international acclaim, renowned in its own right,
Whether Religion, Retail, Family, Friends or the Kids,
Nearly all seem to say, "***...but it's Christmas time!***"

I fell into this trap, but now I finally realise,
There's a loophole created, used for more harm than good,
Mainly concealing individual and collective weakness and lies,
Trade Description violation, because a chip is not a spud.

"*But it derives from it.*" "*Why does it?*" "*I don't know, it just does.*"
We've already taken the bait, like the fish on the hook,
Caught up in it, yet none the wiser, occupied with the fuss,
So, now that you have a minute, why don't we take a look...

Apparently, Christmas is decorations, a tree, lights, seasonal cheer,
Cards, hand-picked presents, kissing under the mistletoe,
Jesus' birthday, carols, Santa, little elves and reindeer,
A play set in Bethlehem, an increased chance of snow.

The list could go on and on, but won't in this case,
I intend to show more than the popular image,
Some, by now, must think I need putting in my place,
As again I hear the repetitive slogan, "***...but it's Christmas!***"

No brainwashing ta, my view comes from my own perception,
And you'll forgive me if I choose not to lose all reason,
The mind is sacred and many need some form of redemption,
From many things, including the illusion of this wintry festive season.

I'm not suggesting for one moment that we shouldn't have fun,
But should observe what these untraceable traditions promote,
Adopted without question, by practically everyone,
Regardless of your beliefs about the Father, Son & Holy Ghost.

People, I'm not judging, but what's with the over-indulgence,
Excessive smoking and boozing, inherent recklessness,

Greater selfishness, via annually intensified expectations,
Feeling obliged to get this and that, thus worsening your debts?!

Blowing at least a months wages in the space of a week,
Wolfing down mounds of fatty and sugary foods,
Turkey, Sheep, Pigs, remember, you are what you eat,
Driving later, but washing it down with stacks of booze.

That rare trip to see your relatives for a brief visit,
On the curiosity of whether they have bought you a present,
If they did, then fingers crossed it's what you WANT, grab paper, rip it,
If not, fake a smile, while inside hiding bitter resentment.

"If we bought a gift for them, we deserve one back, don't we?!"
"No." Plus even when empty handed, you wait with stretched arms,
Not to give them a loving hug, much to the contrary,
Instead, we value how much people care by what they place in our palms.

What wonderful morals we deem to pass on to the Children,
Is this sullenness and greed to be maintained forever?
Like microwaveable meals, the heat and pressure builds under the film,
What happened to simplicity and making magic and memories together?!

Everything is put on hold, while we watch trash on TV,
We can't miss this repetitive viewing, slaves to the channel menu,
Glued to films we've seen 20 times and also have on DVD,
Then pay four times the norm or more for admission at a venue.

It's crazy what we put up with and the pressure we put ourselves through,
Did you know the suicide rate doubles during this time,
Don't let me get started on what corporations convince us to do,
We need to quit this stupid nonsense… and reclaim our lives.

Why do we act insane simply 'cause others say we should?
Why do certain things like Christmas, stop us from thinking straight?
Why are most folk bullied into doing things they don't want to?
Why get into debt and suffer, simply for traditions sake?

Why do people wait for New Year to quit bad habits and stuff?
"What's your New Year's Resolution?" "Sorry, I'm sorted already!"
"But you've gotta have something, it's the New Year, YOU MUST!!!"
It seems to me, that you haven't yet understood the message!

Concrete Parasite Or Paradise?

I close my eyes as a means of travel,
Standing before a red haze, that fades to black,
My portal opens and images start to unravel,
First to appear crisply, is a green blade of grass.

This begins to shrink as my view zooms out,
Now I see millions, all spread before me,
Swaying in the wind, like they're dancing about,
Around a gigantic tree, with light green and khaki leaves.

Just then I heard a voice, ***"I've been expecting you"***,
Loud and bold, at first I thought I'd imagined what I'd heard,
But as I looked closer, the tree began to move,
And smiled at me, quite rightly, I was lost for words.

"Come closer", with caution, I made my way forward,
It picked me up gently and placed me on its shoulders,
I felt like the boy in 'The Never-ending Story',
Enchanted, amazed and wishing it would never be over.

"See all this before you", I answered "yes",
"It's Mother Nature, for a long time now she hasn't been respected,

We too are part of her, and she's being put to death,
Because the laws of preservation are currently being neglected."

"What can be done?" I asked *"okay, but I think you know,*
It's only a matter of time before all life on Earth's extinct,
This beauty will die a cruel death, without resolve, unless you go,
Spread the message, use only what you need and recycle things.

Plus stop building solidified earth monstrosities on animal's homes,
If you must, use empty monstrosities and simply renew them,
Warn all humans, examples of natural beauty must be left alone,
Or Mother Nature will fight back ferociously, again and again.

Stop using toxic substances and creating harmful waste,
Walk and cycle more instead of choosing convenience,
Take pollutive systems and put eco-friendly ones in their place,
A few of the things that will help nature, including human beings.

Another important factor is the energy we generate inside us,
This will help Gaia, providing the strength to heal and live,
Only positive thoughts and actions will ensure the Earth's survival,
But at the moment, a much greater amount of negative exists.

I've said enough, goodbye." I returned in a blink,
And with great urgency, I began my mission,
Spreading the message digitally, verbally and also in ink,
To anyone I could reach, anyone who would listen.

But I couldn't reach everyone or share it fast enough though,
Still worth the effort, as shortly after, it had done some good,
But to succeed you should do the same and those that you know,
Increase awareness, evolve your lifestyle, and ensure it's understood…

That it's crucial and essential that we all play our part,
Even if from the neck downwards, we are paralysed,
The answer lies in our minds, our hands and our hearts,
Shall we feed this Concrete Parasite or return to Paradise?

The World Is So Cold...

Nose hairs breaking like icicles,
Take a deep breath and feel the sting,
Frozen solid, no sniffs or trickles,
That's how cold the World really is.

Worse than the strongest blizzards,
Just think of the total opposite to,
The preferred temperature of an African Lizard,
Timesed by infinity, and you still have no clue.

There is no scientific explanation or theory,
Although there's a reason, which remains hidden,
I try to speak out, but no-one hears me,
The words won't travel, because it's so bitter.

Limbs filled with death, no likely repair,
No new blood arrives, no spent blood can leave,
Resulting in a loss of feeling, as if nothing's there,
Like the black foot of Longfellow Deeds.

Should it be forgotten? Is it still 'there'?
I mourn its condition and try to revive it,
Will nobody help me?! Does anyone care?
Greedy Zombies have no real way of realising.

The weather's preset, forecast, misleading,
This used to be my real smile, and is still what it looks like,
But it's simply frozen to resemble it, that's the reason,
Why the World is so cold... yet still... I smile!

Grateful

The World is so cold, yet still I smile,
An echo of my esoteric, multi-layered meaning,
So I'll give you some additional insight into why,
Not a full moon, but more than the usual gleaming.

My unhappiness is encased in a smile, it's true,
So many known causes and no known cure,
Harsh realities remain undisclosed, but for a few,
All you see is a wide smile and a heart that is pure.

Not the scars, injuries, torment, cuts and bruises,
Mostly out of my hands, so I have scarce regrets,
It seems that whichever way things occur, someone loses,
Like the scientific theory of the butterfly effect...

And I'd rather twist my own umbilical cord first,
Before adding to the suffering of anyone else,
For universal happiness, I'd seesaw a double curse,
For the gift to be unmissed, the curse must balance itself out.

Okay, enough of the riddling, time for some details,
Illuminating shadows, cast on my surface and in craters,
The track must be aligned, to stop me from being derailed,
Because I'm tired of thinking not yet, never or later.

For much of my life, I've been outcast by most,
There, but not welcome, different, an apparent outsider,
My certificate of acceptance, still lost in the post,
The culprits behind this don't want any proof or reminder.

I was bullied as a kid, chased, forced to fight,
Not all the time, but enough to reinforce the last para',
They should've known better, some 4 years older than I,
The only one in my corner throughout was my Moma.

Still, I didn't want to burden her with every bad experience,
She did all she could for me, and does to this day,
Her childhood was worse than mine, with parental negligence,
Malnutrition, abuse, bullying and much more I won't say.

My Father was a Moth disguised as a Butterfly,
Although rarely seen at all, comfortable only in darkness,
Undetected, he would consume happiness, like a black hole does light,
Even if I'd known his crimes, I think he'd of continued regardless.

Does that make me half a man? ...thankfully not!
He died in my early teens, so did my Uncle 3 months prior,
Such raw emotions to deal with, such pain and loss,
My family grew more distant, who'll get Burns from the fire?

My teachers didn't make the link between this and my behaviour,
Instead I'm labelled a lost cause, a waste of their time,
Frequently my Moma had to come and be my saviour,
They were reluctant to listen, the frustration had me crying.

I made it through, but not without detentions, limitations,
The dark thoughts that crossed my mind, were really quite frightening,
So I began writing poetry, to vent the tensions,
It's amazing, the therapeutic effect of a little bit of writing.

Not a cure, but it made things much more bearable,
Plus gave me hope that things would improve, "something's gotta give!"
I touched on private issues, though I didn't share them all,
It gave me a tool to use my pain to try to think positive.

That's what I try to do nowadays, deflect pessimism,
Strive to think for the best, even if it pains me,
Smile in the face of bullies, misery, criticism,
And it's mad, it's them, but should be me who can't take it.

Remember, no matter how harsh your life does get,
At least one other person has it a whole lot harder,
Like losing 3 generations of your family and being close to death,
Because of the Bhopal Disaster, caused by Union Carbide…

And seeing no real compensation, after suffering 20 years,
Plus there are those who lost everything in Tsunami tragedies,
Just think, you could be in a situation worse than your darkest fears,
So count your blessings, not your mistakes, scars or catastrophes.

Not Really Worth My Time!

Tip-tap, tip-tap, tip-tap, tip-tap,
The continual motion of stepping feet,
For your leisure, health or maybe a task,
Going somewhere specific or wherever they lead.

I like walking, it's fun, I can't get enough,
To Town and back, around parks and attractions,
I'm a lone soldier, leaving footprints in the mud,
I prefer it to tedious forced interactions.

You know, when you see an old acquaintance or friend,
Who you'd contact, but would never or rarely reply,
Except when needing a favour, then they'd pretend,
They've always had your back, well, I'd rather walk by...

Than waste my time on exchanging some empty pleasantries,
Instead, I'll use the time saved doing something productive,
Exciting, overdue, like writing this poem, indeed,
For freshness in the home, you have to take out the rubbish.

Ahh, that's a bit cleaner... whoops, I missed a bit...
I hate it when I organise something in advance,
For my friends, and loads of them are up for it,
Then on the day, "...*can't make it...*" "yeah!? ...well, thanks!"

I shouldn't be surprised by now, but still am a little,
As I even give them reminders, plus make it easy and cheap,
Buy extra supplies, entertainment, food, and I'm very hospitable,
But it still takes a miracle for them to come and see me!

At first, I thought it was me, and used to blame myself,
Did whatever it took and gave in to their demands,
When back 'home', I'd visit, visit, visit and nothing else,
The amount they visited me, you'd think I'd moved to Japan!

(J:) Domo arigato gozaimas! (E.T:) Thank you very much!
It's only 20-odd miles, I'm a liddorl kung-fused,
The UK's 2nd largest city, with regular trains and buses,
Regional travel pass under £5, lots to see and do.

Yet most still haven't even seen the house I live in,
It's madness, for almost 2 years I've been staying here,
My enthusiasm's worn off, I mean, you must be kidding?!
The scales are far from balanced, it's hardly been fair.

So I'll take a load off, until things are rectified,
Stay over here relaxing and we'll see if I'm missed,
I've already seen a panic start, some are petrified,
'Cause if the issue isn't resolved, I won't even be pissed.

I'm having tonnes of fun making each moment count,
Doing loads of the things I've wanted to do all along,
There are exceptional people, only a small amount,
But the majority know to which category they belong.

It's their loss, more than mine, I'm the major contributor,
Never caring about me as much as I did about them,
I'd rather someone who holds it down, consistently mutual,
Than a neglectful friend, conveni-buddy or a loose hem.

Sometimes But A Shadow

Am I transparent? I'd like to think I'm not,
Okay, maybe translucent, as I can be kind of dark,
But I'm always able to let a light shine through,
Yeah, I think it's fitting, sure, translucent will do…

Or maybe a shadow, I can't make up my mind,
All I know is I feel invisible most of the time,
I know that I exist, others seem to as well,
Although I disappear in an instant, like during a cloaking spell.

It's weird and can be wonderful, although it doesn't always work,
As sometimes I want to be, yet I'm left looking like a jerk,
On occasions, my actions may leave a few people startled,
But you'll rarely see my cheeks the colour of ripe tomatoes.

From wall to wall I creep, linked to almost everything,
I am always somewhere close, even if not seen,
Or just not focused on, attention stays on the objects,
I receive little appreciation, eventually causing problems.

However, there are a few people, possessing the gifted vision,
To see me objectively and in my other form with precision,
Still not a full understanding, but that's half the beauty,
Constant attention to detail, committed to an unspoken duty.

We've so many great memories, that they smile at my mention,
Plus they appreciate my influence on illustrating dimensions,
We do this for the love, not the potential prizes,
Fishermen selfish... tuppence, A True Friend... Priceless!

About The Author

Following Whispers is the poet and author alias of an English writer who is new to the publishing process, he has however been writing poetry for over two decades. He was initially inspired to put pen to paper after a series of difficult events that shook him to the core, leaving him struggling to make sense of what had happened and why; make sense of the somewhat merciless world around him; his emotions; who he was; and more importantly, who he wanted to become.

Growing up, he didn't really have any conventional male role models around, there was no masculine go-to, someone to encourage him to keep any excessive displays of masculinity in check, or at least help in steering his vessel away from impending destructive outcomes, instead

he was forced to make his own mistakes and find his own feet as a man. This actually ended up working to his advantage, as being raised solely by his Mother afforded him with a sensitive, sensuous side he could tap into when favourable conditions were present. He found that by embracing this feminine side of his personality, he found greater strength of character and clarity of vision.

Whispers is a self-confessed Geek, speaking with him, you find that his thought process is deep but not overwhelming, instead his perspective is inherently heart-warming; intuitive; sometimes dark, but seemingly honest; fun; passionate and inspiring.

When describing his 'voice' and his fondness for writing, he mused, *"I realised that beauty could be born out of not only love, but also pain and other motivations. The more I used this therapeutic implement, the more I realised that it helped me to find a silver lining in even the darkest emotions, experiences, observations and topics; find positivity even in the face of extreme negativity; find strength when I was being forced to feel weak; and find hope that my tomorrows would be brighter."*

It is a safe to say that this will surely not be the last we will hear from this talented poet, and think that another dose of his silver lined musings cannot come soon enough!

If you would like any further information or have a query related to this author or his work, please visit **followingwhispers.com** where you will find his blog, plus details and links for all of his social media profiles, so that you can follow him and enjoy his micro-poetry and other creative pieces.

www.ingramcontent.com/pod-product-compliance
Lightning Source LLC
Chambersburg PA
CBHW071024080526
44587CB00015B/2487